First World War
and Army of Occupation
War Diary
France, Belgium and Germany

36 DIVISION
Divisional Troops
Divisional Cyclist Company
4 October 1915 - 28 June 1916

WO95/2496/2

The Naval & Military Press Ltd
www.nmarchive.com
Published in association with The National Archives

Published by

The Naval & Military Press Ltd

Unit 10 Ridgewood Industrial Park,

Uckfield, East Sussex,

TN22 5QE England

Tel: +44 (0) 1825 749494

www.naval-military-press.com

www.nmarchive.com

This diary has been reprinted in facsimile from the original. Any imperfections are inevitably reproduced and the quality may fall short of modern type and cartographic standards.

© Crown Copyright
Images reproduced by permission of The National Archives, London, England, 2015.

Contents

Document type	Place/Title	Date From	Date To
Heading	WO95/2496/2		
Heading	36th Division Divl Troops 36th Divl Cyclist Coy. Oct 1915-June 1916		
Heading	36th Divl Cyclist Oct Nov Dec 1915 Vol 1, 2, 3 Jan 16		
War Diary	Le Havre	04/10/1915	04/10/1915
War Diary	Longeau	05/10/1915	06/10/1915
War Diary	Flesselles	06/10/1915	20/10/1915
War Diary	Domart En Ponthieu	21/10/1915	26/10/1915
War Diary	Domart	27/10/1915	13/11/1915
War Diary	Domart En Ponthieu	14/11/1915	14/11/1915
War Diary	Mailly Maillet	14/11/1915	15/11/1915
War Diary	Trenches	15/11/1915	16/11/1915
War Diary	Mailly Maillet	15/11/1915	24/11/1915
War Diary	Mailly Maillet	21/11/1915	24/11/1915
War Diary	Domart En Ponthieu	14/11/1915	24/11/1915
War Diary	Domart	26/11/1915	28/11/1915
War Diary	Pont Remy (Somme)	28/11/1915	12/12/1915
War Diary	Pont Remy	14/12/1915	25/12/1915
War Diary		14/12/1915	31/12/1915
Heading	36th Cyclist Vol 4, 5 Feb		
War Diary	Pont. Remy	04/01/1916	04/01/1916
War Diary	Domart En Ponthieu	04/01/1916	18/01/1916
War Diary	Bernaville	18/01/1916	28/01/1916
War Diary	Bernaville (lens 11 1/100000 Ref. Map)	29/01/1916	07/02/1916
War Diary	Mailly Mailly	08/02/1916	11/02/1916
War Diary	Varennes	12/02/1916	29/02/1916
War Diary	Varennes (Ref Map Lens II 1/100000)	29/02/1916	04/03/1916
War Diary	Hedauville	05/03/1916	31/03/1916
War Diary	Hedauville Reference Map Lens II 1/100000		
War Diary	Hedauville		
War Diary	Hedauville Ref Map St. D.S.E. France 1:200000	01/04/1916	10/04/1916
War Diary	St Ouen Ref Map Amiens 12 1:80000	11/04/1916	11/04/1916
War Diary	St Riquier	12/04/1916	18/04/1916
Heading	36 Div Cyclists Vol 6		
War Diary	Martainville Ref Map. Abbeville 1:800000	19/04/1916	19/04/1916
War Diary	Bourdon Ref Map Amiens 12 1:80000	26/04/1916	26/04/1916
War Diary	Varennes	26/04/1916	29/04/1916
War Diary	Appendix 1 To April 1915		
War Diary	Appendix II To April 1916		
War Diary	Appendix 3 To April 1916		
War Diary	Varennes	01/05/1916	31/05/1916
War Diary	Varennes	01/06/1916	30/06/1916
War Diary		01/06/1916	28/06/1916

WO 95/2496/2

36TH DIVISION
DIVL. TROOPS

36TH DIVL CYCLIST COY.
OCT 1915-JUNE 1916

36 Birk: Eyeliss
N

Oct Nov Dec 1915) vol 1, 2, 3. B.
Jan 1916 }
June 16

Army Form C. 2118.

WAR DIARY
or
INTELLIGENCE SUMMARY.
(Erase heading not required.)

Instructions regarding War Diaries and Intelligence Summaries are contained in F. S. Regs., Part II. and the Staff Manual respectively. Title pages will be prepared in manuscript.

Place	Date	Hour	Summary of Events and Information	Remarks and references to Appendices
Le HAVRE	Oct 4th 1915	8 a.m.	Disembarkation at Le Havre of 36th Divl Cyclist Coy. Proceeded to Rest Camp No. 5 where the night was spent under canvas.	J.P.
LONGEAU	Oct 5th 1915	1 p.m.	Entrained for LONGEAU, two miles E. of AMIENS.	
	Oct 6th 1915		Reached LONGEAU at 1.30 a.m. Company then cycled via Amiens to FLESSELLES, leaving distant artillery on the way. Transport reached FLESSELLES 6.30 a.m. about 2 hrs after the platoons.	
FLESSELLES	Oct 6th – Oct 10th		Company made familiar with positions of the various Brigade & Batt. H/qts in Divl. area by means of cycle rides under platoon commanders or N.C.Os.	J.P.

WAR DIARY
INTELLIGENCE SUMMARY

Army Form C. 2118.

Place	Date	Hour	Summary of Events and Information	Remarks and references to Appendices
FLESSELLES	Oct 11th 1915	9.30 a.m.	Coy inspected by G.O.C & complimented for smart appearance. Morning spent in Coying out a tactical exercise (Adv. Guard scheme) proposed & supervised by the G.O.C.	
"	Oct 11th		Company fully warned of the seriousness of offences against discipline on active service. Recent C.M. awards read out to assembled Coy, etc. Importance of taking sanitary precautions, of continually examining gas helmets etc.	
"	Oct 14 - 20		Two Div: Field days held during this period.	
DOMART-en-PONTHIEU	Oct 21st 1915 - Oct 26 1915.		Coy cycled at 9. a.m. to DOMART-en-Ponthieu to take up new quarters. Men warned of prevalence of Rheumal Disease in area. Coy engaged largely on fatigues with the object of improving the sanitary arrangements of billets, but from the 26th Oct onward a considerable portion of	G.O

Army Form C. 2118.

WAR DIARY
or
INTELLIGENCE SUMMARY
(Erase heading not required.)

Place	Date	Hour	Summary of Events and Information	Remarks and references to Appendices
DOMART	Oct 27th		each day was devoted to physical exercise musketry bombing & bayonet fighting (with or without gas helmets). Employed every help to ensure that each man had his gas helmet fit for use in a gas-attack.	
	60th 28th 1915		Div l Tactical exercise. Cyclist platoons, scattered over a wide area, averaged withdrawn to a common point by well-timed retirements & skilful intercommunication. C.O.'s twice awarded umpire's decisions when establishing contact with superior forces. Twelve finals found to be useless for writing messages on wet days. Officers & N.C.O's warned to provide themselves with ordinary pencils for future field Days.	B.P.

WAR DIARY
or
INTELLIGENCE SUMMARY.
(Erase heading not required.)

Army Form C. 2118.

Place	Date	Hour	Summary of Events and Information	Remarks and references to Appendices
DOMART	Oct 28th to Nov 7th		NOVEMBER. Nothing of importance to report. Routine work, with occasional foot route-march. A cycle route-match can be very trying to men who are not riding in front, that only those the roads to be watched, but one attention is for the most part taken up in watching the rear mud-guard of the man in front. On wet days there is always the danger of skidding; on dry days, dust is plentiful. For these reasons an occasional foot-march is always popular. It would be absurd for a platoon to attempt to sing on a cycle route march.	
	Nov 11th		Six reinforcements arrived from A.C.C. depôt.	BR
	Nov 12th & 13th		Usual parades.	

WAR DIARY
or
INTELLIGENCE SUMMARY.

Army Form C. 2118.

Place	Date	Hour	Summary of Events and Information	Remarks and references to Appendices
DOMART-en-Ponthieu	Nov. 14th 1915.		The C.O. (Capt. Warman), 2nd Lieuts Scott & Stephens, Co. & S. Major Charlton & 64 N.C.O's & men paraded at 6.45 a.m. for the purpose of proceeding to the trenches near Mailly Maillet. Still weather was intensely cold & snow was falling heavily when the parade moved off. Packs being very heavy & weather conditions adverse, two long halts had to be made to enable stragglers to catch up. The total length of the ride (via Rubempcourt, Talmas, Puchvillers, Rancheval, Achent, Forceville) was about 26 miles. Mailly was reached at 1 p.m. The nights of the 14th & 15th was passed in billets at Mailly.	
MAILLY MAILLET	Nov. 15th 1915.	1 p.m.	Party moved off after breakfast to the trenches, where they were met by the guides. [Sick men were left at Mailly & guard stores]. Capt. Warman, 2 Lt. Scott & 30 men were led to the portion of the line, held by the Seaforths. The remainder under 2 Lt. Stephens were led to that the sector	S.L.

WAR DIARY or INTELLIGENCE SUMMARY

Army Form C. 2118.

Place	Date	Hour	Summary of Events and Information	Remarks and references to Appendices
Mailly Maillet Trenches	15th & 16th 1915		On the immediate right of the 2nd Batt. Seaforths then held by the 1st Warwicks, the line were comparatively quiet. We were informed that the troops opposite to were Saxons. The enemy snipers were active in the day time when the fog lifted. Two of the Warwicks were shot through the head, a few yards away from our men, but our only casualts were Cyclist W Barry [594 2] of the 4 Platoon. When trying to locate a sniper, his eyepiece was struck by an explosive bullet. Some glass + lead pierced his skull. He was stunned for about 10 mins but was then able to walk to the nearest Dressing Station. The chief dangers were the snipers & at night the machine guns which occasionally swept the parapets. The German trenches were about 150 yards away down a slope. Each 18 own platoons held about 100 yds of fire trenches for about 48 hrs	E.P.

Army Form C. 2118.

WAR DIARY
or
INTELLIGENCE SUMMARY
(Erase heading not required.)

Instructions regarding War Diaries and Intelligence Summaries are contained in F. S. Regs., Part II. and the Staff Manual respectively. Title pages will be prepared in manuscript.

Place	Date	Hour	Summary of Events and Information	Remarks and references to Appendices
Mailly Maillet	Nov 15th & 16th 1915		On the 15th nations were issued, & on both days there were several degrees of frost. The Cyclists were very hospitably received by both Officers & men of the Seaforths & Warwicks, a circumstance which kept everybody cheerful during a very trying time.	
	Nov. 17th		At 9 a.m. on the 17th, being relieved, the Cyclists returned to Mailly Maillet, via the Sunken. In the village they were met by the second detachment of Cyclists for the trenches under the command of Lieut. J. R. M. Marlow. This detachment was composed mainly of No. 2 Platoon under 2nd Lieut. N. McKeown & No. 5 Platoon under 2nd Lieut. C. R. Earsange Johnston — in all,	JP

2353 Wt. W2544/1454 700,000 5/15 D. D. & L. A.D.S.S./Forms/C. 2118.

Place	Date	Hour	Summary of Events and Information	Remarks and references to Appendices
NAILLY MAILLET	Nov. 19th to 20		C.H. 7h C.O's 9 men under the above-mentioned three Officers. Lieut. Marlow, 2nd Lieut. McKown, of No. 2 platoon were attached to the 1st Warwicks, 2nd Lieut. Johnston, No. 5 Platoon, to the 2nd Seaforths. The experiences of the men were similar to those of the first detachment except that the enemy sent over a few minenwerfer shells sufficiently near to blow out the candles in the dug-outs. The Officers showed no lack of pluck; the men carried out their duties enthusiastically during the three days in which they remained in the front-line area. There were no casualties.	

Army Form C. 2118.

WAR DIARY
or
INTELLIGENCE SUMMARY.
(Erase heading not required.)

Place	Date	Hour	Summary of Events and Information	Remarks and references to Appendices
MAILLY -MAILLET	Nov 21st /915. — Nov 24th /915		The Third & final detachment of Cyclists arrived in Mailly about noon, Nov. 21st. They were under the command of Lieut. R. Hammar, who had come up mainly for instruction in cyphers. His officer was attached to the 1st Batt. Rifle Brigade, but unfortunately the facilities offered for instruction were not very great. The Hama had to rely chiefly on his own initiative & previous knowledge of musketry. The two platoons under 2 Lieut. Gimbey did not take over a part of the line but were engaged on arduous & at times dangerous fatigue duties. These consisted in making barbed wire cages during the day time & carrying them to the fire trenches by night. During the	90

Place	Date	Hour	Summary of Events and Information	Remarks and references to Appendices
MAILLY-MAILLET	Nov 21st Nov. 24th 1915		day, nine trestles were brought up "over the top", under cover of fog. Occasionally when wire was being brought "over the top" at night a star shell would reveal the presence of the working party & a machine gun would open fire. The men, however, always fell instinctively on their faces & there were no casualties to record.	
DOMART EN-PONTHIEU	14-11-1915 to 24-11-1915		NOTE: From Nov. 14th – Nov. 24th the rest of the Co'y. were engaged in ordinary routine work at Domart.	

WAR DIARY
INTELLIGENCE SUMMARY

Army Form C. 2118.

Place	Date	Hour	Summary of Events and Information	Remarks and references to Appendices
DOMART	26/11/1915		Advanced party of 2 N.C.O's & 6 men sent to new billeting area, Pont-Remy (Somme) Party to perform Guard duties until arrival of company	
	Nov 27th 1915	8.30 a.m.	Sentence of 14 days F.P. No 1 on Cadet No 1919 P.A. Doughty awarded by F.G.C.M. 8/11/15 has been quashed by order of Commander 3rd Army on grounds of illegality — Authority Telegram No. D.A./26 4 of 23/11/15	
PONT-REMY (Somme)	Nov 28th 1915	1.15 a.m.	Co. forwarded to proceed to new billeting area, Pont-Remy (Somme)	
	Nov 28th to 29/30/1915	7 PM	General fatigues, principally sanitary work. Unloading Mobile Disinfecting Artillery Thro' shifts. Flour an 6 W Two Platoons to a shift	S.P. f. W.

WAR DIARY
INTELLIGENCE SUMMARY.
(Erase heading not required.)

Army Form C. 2118.

Place	Date	Hour	Summary of Events and Information	Remarks and references to Appendices
PONT-REMY (Somme)	5.12.15		**DECEMBER** The following letter was received:- "The Divisional Commander wishes me to inform you that he is very pleased to learn from the Staff Officer Commanding the detraining of the Ulster Artillery, of the excellent work performed and the most adverse conditions by the Cyclist Company who are reported to have carried out their duties in the most efficient & cheery manner. (signed) J. Lowyn A.A. & Q.M.G."	
	7.12.15		The Coy moved to billets at J.15 D.1. Artillery	
	10.12.15 -12.12.15		The Coy moved to the entrainment J.15. 36.D.1. Artillery (T.F.)	

Army Form C. 2118.

WAR DIARY
or
INTELLIGENCE SUMMARY.
(Erase heading not required.)

Instructions regarding War Diaries and Intelligence Summaries are contained in F. S. Regs., Part II. and the Staff Manual respectively. Title pages will be prepared in manuscript.

Place	Date	Hour	Summary of Events and Information	Remarks and references to Appendices
PONT REMY	14.1.15.		— A dinner was given by the Officers to the C.O. to mark the first anniversary of the Coy's formation.	
			— The following letter was rec'd from H.Q. "The General Officer Commanding is very pleased to learn from the Divisional Commander Staff Officers of the excellent work done by the Officers N.C.Os & men of the 36th Divisional Cyclists during the training movement of the 26th Divisional Artillery to On training (T.F.)	
	19.1.15		— a concert was given by the Coy to the troops in the "Anse" lg. g. arm.	

Army Form C. 2118.

WAR DIARY
or
INTELLIGENCE SUMMARY.
(Erase heading not required.)

Instructions regarding War Diaries and Intelligence Summaries are contained in F. S. Regs., Part II. and the Staff Manual respectively. Title pages will be prepared in manuscript.

Place	Date	Hour	Summary of Events and Information	Remarks and references to Appendices
PONTREMY	25.12.15		The men paraded for Church in new huts	
	14 — 31	11.15	Training continues as usual, chiefly Battery manning, sword exercise, Each week a tactical scheme on Canvas and in conjunction with the Cavalry Squadron. C.S.S. C.S. have killed Dragoon, who has been (answer poulticed) the property of the Bn. No. 1 Troop, 1st Div. since March 1915 when the squadron stayed at Enniskillen. Slaughtered together at Enniskillen.	

36th Cyclus
bl. 4, 5

Feb

Army Form C. 2118.

WAR DIARY
or
INTELLIGENCE SUMMARY.
(Erase heading not required.)

Instructions regarding War Diaries and Intelligence Summaries are contained in F. S. Regs., Part II. and the Staff Manual respectively. Title pages will be prepared in manuscript.

Place	Date	Hour	Summary of Events and Information	Remarks and references to Appendices
PONT REMY			JANUARY	
			Training continued	
	4.1.16		The Coy. moved to DOMART EN PONTHIEU	
DOMART EN PONTHIEU	18.1.16		The Coy moved to BERNAVILLE.	
BERNAVILLE	24.1.16		Tactical Exercise with Squadron + one + two	
	26.1.16		Infantry Battalions	
	28.1.16			

Army Form C. 2118.

WAR DIARY
or
INTELLIGENCE SUMMARY.
(Erase heading not required.)

Sheet 1

Place	Date	Hour	Summary of Events and Information	Remarks and references to Appendices
BERNAVILLE LENS 11 1/100000 & MAP.	29/1/1916 to 1/2/1916		Nothing to Report.	
do	2/2/1916		Tactical Exercises with Divisional Enemy	
do	3/2/1916 to 6/2/1916		Company moved to MAILLY-MAILLET. Company took over Road Control posts at 9.30 am from 4th Division. (49 men under A.P.M.)	
do	7/2/1916		Nothing to Report.	
MAILLY-MAILLT.	8/2/16			
do	9/2/16		Attached to 150th Coy R.E. from this date 3 NCO & 25 men. 76th Sanitary Section from this date 1 NCO & 9 men. B. & Canteen from this date. 3 men.	

Army Form C. 2118.

WAR DIARY
or
INTELLIGENCE SUMMARY.
(Erase heading not required.)

Sheet 2

Place	Date	Hour	Summary of Events and Information	Remarks and references to Appendices
MAILLY-MAILLY	10/2/1916		Nothing to Report	
do	11/2/1916		Company moved to VARENNES	
VARENNES	12/2/1916 to 14/2/1916		Nothing to report	
do	15/2/1916		Company took over two Observation Posts situated at Q 22 d 82 & Q 9 b/01 Ref Map 1:20,000 57D SE.	
do	16/2/1916 to 29/2/16		Nothing to report	

For Disposition of Coy at date see Appendices attd. No. 1.

W M Warren Capt
O/c 36th Div Cyclist Coy

Army Form C. 2118.

WAR DIARY
or
INTELLIGENCE SUMMARY.
(Erase heading not required.)

Place	Date	Hour	Summary of Events and Information	Remarks and references to Appendices

VARENNES Ref Map LENS II 1/100000	29/1/1916		Appendices to February 1916
			 Nº 1
			 Disposition of 36 Div Cyclist Coy 29/1/1916
			 Attaches to:— Off. O.R.
			 36 Div. H.Q. Officers &c 1 25
			 36 Div School 1 3
			 " A.D.C. (Guards) — 1
			 " R.T.O. Failhas — 1
			 " Signal Coy — 12
			 " A.P.M. Police)
			            Couriers) — 54
			 76th Sanitary Section — 10
			 150th Coy R.E. — 28
			 Observation Post — 14
			 13th Corps HQ — 1
			 Town Commdt Harang — 1
			 Company 6 48
			                                 8 194
			
			 W Wannan Capt
			 O.C. 36th Div. Cyclist Coy	

Army Form C. 2118.

WAR DIARY
or
INTELLIGENCE SUMMARY.
(Erase heading not required.)

Instructions regarding War Diaries and Intelligence Summaries are contained in F.S. Regs., Part II. and the Staff Manual respectively. Title pages will be prepared in manuscript.

Sheet 1

Place	Date	Hour	Summary of Events and Information	Remarks and references to Appendices
VARENNES Reference MAP LENS 11. 1/100,000	1/3/1916 to 3/3/1916		Nothing to report.	
do	4/3/1916		Company moved to HEDAUVILLE.	
HEDAUVILLE	5/3/1916.		Road Control Posts (under A.P.M.) rejoined Company this date. (Nos. 1, 2 & 3) = 21 men. Road Control Posts Nos. 5 & 7 rejoined Company this date = 14 men.	
do	6/3/1916. to 14/3/1916		Nothing to report	
do	15/3/1916		Two detachments on Road Control Posts rejoined the Company this date = 14 men	
do	16/3/16 to 19/3/16		Nothing to report	

2353 Wt. W2544/1454 700,000 5/15 D.D. & L, A.D.S.S./Forms/C. 2118.

Army Form C. 2118.

Sheet 2

WAR DIARY
or
INTELLIGENCE SUMMARY.
(Erase heading not required.)

Place.	Date.	Hour.	Summary of Events and Information	Remarks and references to Appendices
HEDAUVILLE	20/3/1916.		A working party of 1 Officer & 30 O.R. instructed to report to 36th Divisional Signal Coy. at the Cemetery on MESNIL - MARTINSART road at 8/30 am. This date was shelled during the morning & compelled to leave off work.	
do	21/3/1916 to 31/3/1916		Nothing to report	

For Allocation of Company see Appendix attd No 1
Report on General Service Cotton bicycle see App. No 2.

M Manna Capt
OC 36th Divisional Cyclist Coy

WAR DIARY or INTELLIGENCE SUMMARY

Army Form C. 2118.
Sheet 3

Place	Date	Hour	Summary of Events and Information	Remarks and references to Appendices
HEDAUVILLE			Reference Map LENS 11 1/100000	

Appendix to March 1916.
No. 1

Allocation of 36th Divisional Cyclist Company.

Attached to:
		Off.	O.R.
36th Div. H.Q.		1	29
36th Div. Details (Officers in)			4
" A.C. Corbie			1
" R.T.O. Railhead			12
" Refnos Coy			4
" A.P.M. Beauvre			10
76th Sanitary Sectn.			26
150th Coy R.E.			16
Sanitation Corps		2	1
137th Corps H.Q.			1
Town Comms. F. MAILLY		1	
" " HEDAUVILLE		1	
Company		3	85
Hospital		1	2
Leave			1
		8	194

W.B. Warnop Capt
O.C. 36th Divisional Cyclist Coy.

WAR DIARY
or
INTELLIGENCE SUMMARY

Army Form C. 2118.

Place	Date	Hour	Summary of Events and Information	Remarks and references to Appendices
HEDAUVILLE			Appendix to March 1916. No. 2. Report on P. Service Pattern Bicycle during trials &c. (a) Some alteration in the service Pattern Bicycle is called for. In the extremely muddy roads & cross country of this area, the Service Bicycle exists in mud & between the war area, & an almost unridable object. The mud gets clogged & almost unridable in the mudguards & brakes at the wheels, clogging in from spokes at the brakes, & the mudguards, exhibited by both mudguards. The primary alterations are hoped to: (1) To clearance of another 1/2" from mudguard to tyre. (2) The substitution of Hub Brakes, (as open) by Bowden wire (Palais Pattern) in both front & back wheels. (c) The front carrier supplies to be for the type attached to the head, body and top light – (d) A 28 × 1 1/2 tyres on Tyre to the tees of the bicycle. A number rather on the faulty make. Tyres supplied (1 1/2 is) hard, are bad in wet mud. The Dunlop Palais & also autumns tyre on light wear.	

36. Army Form C. 2118

Page 2118
Vol 4

WAR DIARY
or
INTELLIGENCE SUMMARY
(Erase heading not required.)

Places	Date	Hour	Summary of Events and Information	Remarks and references to Appendices
HEDAUVILLE	1-10.4.16		Remained 1 Coy. not employed elsewhere constructed 6.5 dug outs 1 mess 30 x 8'6" 1 priv 6 x 9 at 932082 – HARTINSART-ENGELBELMER Rd. for occupation of personnel of O.P's during plenary moon. – Also new O.P at 9.16d.86	Ref map 57D.S.E. France 1:20,000
STOUEN	11.4.16		The Coy moved to ST. OUEN and were attm to join the MEERUT Brigade 2nd Indian Cavalry Divin for a march of 133 days having with cavalry in support of WHITE S.S. 65 hours Cavalry Divisions. For 36th Divn. huts to Spt. arm. This ride, 125 wide was 1 foot had rain poured in severe in our tent who has been absent from the Coy. a various employments which as we going were not being able. The Lieut Colonel Coy. was also billeted in ST OUEN for the day. Coy moved to ST. RIQUIER (15 miles)	Ref hap. Amiens 12. 1:80,000
ST RIQUIER	12.4.16 -18.4.16		Field days	

3/ Du
Cycles
Vol 6
———

WAR DIARY
or
INTELLIGENCE SUMMARY.
(Erase heading not required.)

Army Form C. 2118.

Place	Date	Hour	Summary of Events and Information	Remarks and references to Appendices
MARTAINVILLE Ref. map Amiens 1:80,000	19.4.16		Coy. move to MARTAINVILLE (21 miles). Training with Bayonet assault. Letter from [?] gratefully from having been constantly with a new Division and System (S.S.65 having killed Divisions) since back 1915.	
BOURDON Ref. map 26.4.16 Annex 12 1:80,000			Coy. move to BOURDON (21 miles). 30 C. Cyclist Coy. was billeted in HANGEST-SUR-SOMME for night.	
VARENNES	27.4.16		Coy. move to Varennes (26 miles). The instructions were that there was to be 34.5 hour 9th Coy. (archives) attached) since its formation 17 more [?] yesterday – unless average of one move per fortnight.	
	29.4.16		Personal of 49 Cyclists who has relieved one 9 Coy. Divl. Cyclist [?]	

APPENDIX I to April 1916.

TRANSPORT.

Since coming to France, no more 1 Fd Coy. has been accepted without the addition of 1 MOTOR TRANSPORT lorry to their Transport allotted to the coy. in w. Establishment. This is largely due to the No. of spare bicycles [transport] which has to be carried. This also renders them dependent by the fact that no his kit, there are [rounds] M'Coy wear by ship are called out to perform [duty] however that there have put [cannot] arrive till [maybe] after they have reached there destination. While doing trench warfare such extra transport is generally available. It is true in the time of [...] mover mobile steam warfare.

Appendix II to April 1916

DIVISIONAL SNIPERS.

Since early in March the Bry has called upon privates of the No.1 Snipers (and was chiefly on the front line. Snipers (ws. is separated) were provided. These Snipers took a keen interest & true to their little line. They had rifles and readings. I chiefly on two tactics to which Rice was entrenched. Both claim between 15 deaths each 15 are not so entrenched in the line. During April Rice ammunition was expended by Lt. Hawes & they hope to be successful during the time they were between.

Lt. Hawes & Corp. Addison Cyclists Hudson Peppard attended a course of Sniping Instruction at Fourth Army HQ from April 9th - 16th. Reports attached.

Appendix 3 to April 1916.

MOTOR BICYCLE

Motor Bicycle should be provided until the Service M.T.
O.C. Some transport here is

The same man on which permanents have to be, has also
in the Infantry apply to provision of the
Further the kid's own transfers of the by when it by can
is on the line made a heavy bicycle wanted to be got
by commander if he is to perform all the work asked of
him.

W.O. Newman Capt
O.C. 91st C.E.R

MAY.

Army Form C. 2118.

36 D in Cyclists
Vol 5

WAR DIARY
or
INTELLIGENCE SUMMARY.
(Erase heading not required.)

Place	Date	Hour	Summary of Events and Information	Remarks and references to Appendices
VARENNES	May 1-31			
	May 31.1916		Coy. engaged on Working Parties, etc. for 1st Division. Instr. G. 1 & Q. O.B./1/507 Organisation 1 Divisional Mounted Troops. 15 Company was reorganised from two dates. Half the Coy. were transferred to 15th R. Ir. Rifles. The remaining half became B. Coy. X Corps Cyclist Battalion. Distribution of these transferred to Infantry was as follows.	
			A.P.M. 2	
			D.H.Q. Orderlies ... 7	
			D.H.Q. Clerks 2	
			A hers 2	
			Pollies 3	
			Intelligence Police . 1	
			R.T.O. 1	
			School (Godsby) ... 2	
			C.R.E. 1	
			Sanitary (HQ) 2	
			H.Q. Signallers ... 1	
			B. hers 1	
			Other Orderlies ... 6	
			Canteens 7	
			Signal Coy 20	
			Observation Post .. 14	
			Train Spiral Sirat to Battalion ... 12	
			Total 84	

W.H. Newman Capt.
O.C. 36th Div. Cyclists

Army Form C. 2118.

WAR DIARY
or
INTELLIGENCE SUMMARY.

(Erase heading not required.)

Instructions regarding War Diaries and Intelligence Summaries are contained in F. S. Regs., Part II. and the Staff Manual respectively. Title pages will be prepared in manuscript.

Place	Date	Hour	Summary of Events and Information	Remarks and references to Appendices
VARENNES	1-30.6.16		JUNE	
	1-28		Working Parties.	
	28-30		Coy. took up stations allotted to it during offensive operations.	
			Distribution	O.R.
			Prisoners Escorts	41
			Stragglers Battle P.o.C	21
			Salvage Coy.	3
			Orderlies to from h.qrs.	5
			Corps. Observation Post	1
			Div. Observation Post	2
			Div. Road Reconnaissance	2
			H.Q. (Coy.)	19
				94
				4

M.W. Dunnan Capt.
O.C. 51st... 48th Highland Battalion

www.ingramcontent.com/pod-product-compliance
Lightning Source LLC
Chambersburg PA
CBHW082358170426
43191CB00048B/2084